THE SIBYL CASSANDRA

A Christmas Play with the Insanity and Sanctity of Five Centuries Past

Gil Vicente

Introduction and Translation by

Cheryl Folkins McGinniss

University Press of America,® Inc.
Lanham · New York · Oxford

Copyright © 2000 by
University Press of America,® Inc.

4501 Forbes Boulevard, Suite 200
Lanham, Maryland 20706

12 Hid's Copse Rd.
Cumnor Hill, Oxford OX2 9JJ

All rights reserved

British Library Cataloging in Publication Information Available

Library of Congress Cataloging-in-Publication Data

Vicente, Gil, ca. 1470-ca. 1536
(Auto de la sibila Casandra. English)
The Sibyl Cassandra : a Christmas play with the insanity and sanctity of
five centuries past / Gil Vicente ; introduction and translation by
Cheryl Folkins McGinniss.
p. cm.
Includes bibiographical references and index.
I. McGinniss, Cheryl Folkins. II. Title
PQ9251.S513 2000   869.2'2—dc21   00—042321 CIP

ISBN 0-7618-1773-5 (pbk: alk. ppr)

To my parents, with gratitude,
for cherished Christmas memories

Contents

Preface.

Acknowledgments.

Introduction.

The Play: *The Sibyl Cassandra*..1

Notes...20

Works Cited..24

Index...26

Preface

My attraction to Gil Vicente's Christmas play, *The Sibyl Cassandra*, and my endeavor, now, to "package" it for a wider audience, has been in the making, probably, since my youth. I grew up in a southwestern town where the scorching sun at midday and the icy chill of the moon battled. Contrasts and opposition were desert norms. So too were my familial surroundings, where an apologetic--or defense of faith, was as routine as night and day. My mother, whose heart-felt obedience to Catholicism, and my father, whose use of Scripture to support his inclination toward agnosticism, provided me with a wonderful gift. This gift was the stage upon which I could view and value debate. I grew up watching, as if in a theater, a pageantry of popes and poets whose ideas or doctrines, presented in dramatic fashion, challenged or affirmed religious or societal rules.

Years later, it was no surprise that I should fall in love with the Castilian theater, for the characters were quite familiar. They struggled with opposing forces: oppressive religious expectations and personal desire for liberation. I perceived these characters, especially through the theater of Juan del Encina and Gil Vicente, as a lovable synthesis of rebellious piety. Cassandra, a self-assured and assertive woman who laments her circumstance in life, has always been a favorite character of mine.

My desert youth impacted me in other ways as well. Certainly, I absorbed the warm Hispano/Latino atmosphere of the community, and quite naturally continued to live and breathe with Mexican, or Caribbean or peninsular literature and politics as part of my being. Although I did not realize it at the time, I was beginning to digest the concept of liberation as well. Probably at that instant in which I gladly traded my bland cafeteria meal for a flavor-packed homemade *tortilla con frijoles*, I connected with the migrant community—and ultimately with those whose existence is marginalized. I would savor the promise of liberation theology in the days to come.

In due course, my adventure with formal theology led me to rural Hispanic or Latino communities where I listened to the "voice of the poor." With few exceptions, this voice was a woman's voice who placed her lament in poetry or song. It did not take me long to understand the close bond between liberation theology and feminist theology. Cassandra's voice from Castile did not seem remote. It was a voice, though five-centuries old, that captured a universal plea.

Cassandra's lament is one that resonates with the suffering of anyone who is held bound. I present her case within a context that I hope will lead to discussion or debate. It is through the dramatization of ideas and conflicts that an "actor" is free to walk in another's shoes. I present this play, then, to readers for their active involvement, and for their final verdict: the sanctity or insanity of Cassandra's case.

Acknowledgments

I wish to thank my husband Vince who has supported and encouraged my work, especially through his assistance with the research and interpretation of music found in the archives and back alleys of Spain. I also give thanks to my daughter, Cecilia, who as a recent Ph.D. in Spanish, and with a current knowledge of the Castilian Theater, has generously shared insights, delightful collegial dialogue, and a bawdy laugh. I thank my son Vincent whose wit and subtle humor, especially as they underlie his writing style, align my perspective of Gil Vicente. Charlotte, my daughter, who sings and performs, *is* Cassandra in beauty and spirited-will, and I thank her for using this translation for one of her auditions.

Thanks are in order, also, for Dr. Carolyn Scott, Chair of the English Department at the Pontifical College Josephinum, who has contributed a vision of authenticity with respect to the performance of the *Sibyl Cassandra*. Dr. Scott refers to the sixteenth and seventeenth-century tradition of the masque where the gender and role of a character are identified through the costume or mask, and where the actors are members of the court or the convent or the monastery in which the play is performed.

Introduction

The Sibyl Cassandra in a Contemporary Context

  To miss the season's production of the Nutcracker, the first grade's March of the Magi or a rendition of Scrooge would be--well almost sacrilegious. With Tchaikovsky, Dickens, Bach, Matthew or Luke as backdrops, the nativity is given tribute within a spirit of the season's transforming magic. The divine is made human, the obstinate yields, and the inanimate breathes and twirls through space.

  Today, as in sixteenth-century Spain, Christmas becomes a time for theatrical, poetical, or musical performances that entertain and teach. During this season of Advent, people, as they did centuries ago in Castile, gather within sacred and secular settings to review the themes of: re-birth, conversion, generosity, rejection, restoration, and liberation. In view of this, perhaps the Castilian drama, *The Sibyl Cassandra*, which was presented after Christmas Matins in 1513, could be reviewed and restored into present liturgical or theatrical space as well.[1] This play, with its focus on love, marriage, sacrifice, birth--and heated debate about the role and place of women, might fit quite appropriately into our ancestral trunk. After all, it is from our collected repertoire of rhyme and design that each Christmas is adorned. A contemporary rendition of this delightful play is presented, then, for anyone who may wish to renew, rekindle, or perhaps, reenact, a tradition from the past.

  In as much as the sacred liturgy reenacts and remembers Christ's sacrifice for all, so do we re-create and re-visit the manger each Christmas in many sacred and secular ways. By reviving Gil Vicente's *Sibyl Cassandra*, a medieval style of humor may be re-born as well. This is a humor that allows us to laugh at authority, and more especially, to place ourselves in a more light-hearted perspective. As Vicente's characters support their theological stance with an occasionally inept reference to Scripture, does not comedy lurk within the ranks of present day religious debate? And although Mary, the mother of God, is affirmed, in this play, through her portrayal as a sturdy warrior prepared for battle, is this image not something that we also praise in contemporary heroines? And considering the fact that Cassandra bucks the societal and religious requirements of the times, five centuries later, is this, too, not an isolated stance? The *Sibyl Cassandra*, a play that is both entertaining and didactic, fits well into our present circumstance. It provides a reflection on the political and social climate; it rekindles a spirit of faith, and supplies an embellishment of worship.

Can politics, artistic expression, and the Eucharist be combined through one function and one winter's gathering? If Christian worship embraces a "public speaking, acting, and touching in Christ's name" (White 1991, 90), then, why not? And why could it not be imagined that Vicente's play be presented in conjunction with Christmas Matins--as it was originally? A dramatic reading would suffice, but let not a more authentic rendition deter any group with imagination or choreographic and musical flair.

There is, however, one warning. This play is set upon turbulent grounds, for in it, a woman, Cassandra, rejects the patriarchal systems of the day. She chooses to be neither a wife or nun as sixteenth-century ideology required. She supports her argument from a theological stance--and the only sensible stance left for a refined and intelligent woman with such a strong calling to serve God as single, celibate, and unavowed. Thus, Cassandra maintains that **she** is the Virgin from whom the Child Redeemer will be born.

Cassandra's uncles, the patriarchs Moses, Isaiah and Abraham, and her aunts, patriarchal women who support traditional women's roles, preach the values of reproduction and obedience Ironically, the men, along with Cassandra's suitor Solomon, intensify their argument with the performance of a *folía*, a pagan dance of fertility and solicitation![2] The aunts, whose names, Erutea, Peresica and Cimeria, engender a pagan background, preach in accordance with their birthright of prophet and priest.[3] The secular and the sacred, the biblical and the pagan, the pastoral and the courtly become intertwined and thrust through time warps, and scene and costume changes, until the characters finally witness the birth of Christ.

Does Cassandra eventually conform? Is there compromise by all? That is for the reader and/or the director to decide. Yet, if any profound conversion should occur, it will take place after the play's culminating moment--when a curtain is drawn that reveals the crèche. After all, a fundamental teaching of the Christmas feast is that everything will be renewed and restored through Christ. This nativity scene is highlighted, further, by four angels who sing a lullaby to "our God and Redeemer." Through song, the angels implore the Christ Child not to cry. Tears, they argue, will cause suffering for the Virgin thus contradicting the notion that Mary bears her son without pain.

The puns and plays of opposition continue. Cassandra exclaims she has been lost in this world--a sentiment not uncommon to women whose talent and intellect may be subdued or whose nonconformity may be labeled as insane. It is not surprising, then, that Cassandra never articulates the words: "I do." Nor does Solomon propose anew. The characters simply continue to adore and praise both Child and Mother, and as if biblical shepherds, perform a *chacota*--an exuberant and rustic dance of joy.[4] Conflict and anguish appear, at least, to have been disrupted and tempered through Christ. Even the characters Moses and Isaiah, the once proud and arrogant preachers of God's truth, now humbly ask for Christ's forgiveness (Vicente 1968, 68-69).

Then, as suddenly as God appeared upon the scene, as *deus ex machina*, all of the characters, including the nuns portraying angels, are transferred into a palatial scene. In sets of three, they perform a courtly promenade.[5] Through song and dance, tribute is given to the grace, beauty, and fortitude of women, with Mary, the "mirror of generations," being predominately esteemed. Each patriarch joins hands in dance with two women--a sibyl and an angel. The dance promenade unfolds with courtliness and joy which are sixteenth-century symbols for service of love.[6] The divine and the worldly, the controversial and the typical, laity and religious, the celibate and married, the secular and the sacred, blend harmoniously and ooperatively into one magnificent choreographic plan.

The ensemble reconfigures for one final encore that transforms them into catechists with one departing didactic theme. In the spirit of *"Onward Christian Soldiers,"* they sing of angels who join soldiers on earth to fight for God. In the midst of worldly strife, harmony, balance, equality, and a reciprocity of loving service are all courtly and contemporary Christian gifts.[7]

Perhaps, the true meaning of this play can be more fully understood by assuming a role. Then, as a sibyl, patriarch, lover, dissident, or angelic presence on earth, the "actor" may contemplate his or her perspective and contribution to the piece. Above all, laugh, for I believe that it is in a light-hearted discovery of our truths and folly that we become closer to the divine. And if this vicentine play does not approach even the steps that lead to a more formal liturgical space; perhaps, it could unfold beautifully as a reading in front of the hearth, where family and friends gather during the Christmas season to reinstate and re-envision their place and role in God's world.

The Sibyl Cassandra in its Castilian Setting

The stage is set in the center of Spain, in the region of the *Castillas* as it was known then and today. Within this center of medieval Castile, a Theater began to form whose spirit, from the perspective of a contemporary audience, might seem both blasphemous and holy. This medieval spirit, that is to say, the spirit of Castile, is anchored intellectually and spiritually to the University of Salamanca that was founded in 1218 by King Alfonso IX. It is a spirit that owes its identity to a multitude of influences including Ovid's *Ars Amandi, The Art of Love*; the classical Greek theater with its use of the dance and chorus as an interact or transitional device; Arabic, French and Portuguese poetry that capture the sentiment of a lover's loss, a pilgrimage or holy crusade; and, of course the sacred texts, liturgies, and teachings of the Catholic Church. It is a spirit that stretches the boundaries between piety and an outright flirtation with sin.[8]

This duality of spirit is inherent in the paradox of the Middle Ages, for as Otis Green explains in his time-honored study of *Spain and the Western Tradition*, "truancy and recantation" were seen as an inseparable part of human nature (1968, 6-10). That is to say, sin and divine forgiveness walked hand in hand. Literature, of course, reflected this contradiction, especially with its parody of the sacred (ibid., 7, 36). Poking fun at authority or making light of a religious practice or ceremony provided a comic relief and elicited a delightful laughter from an audience. This is and always will be a part of human nature and dramatic license.

> Such indulgence in levity and in gay parody is essentially respectful, as the child mimicking his parent is respectful and would be terrified by any thought of suppressing parenthood. It is a human phenomenon so diffused through many cultures that any given stance of it seems to have its justification in human nature (ibid., 36).

Parody of the sacred is, indeed, infused within the Castilian Theater. The fact that these productions were performed in convents or courts and before the very people that were being ridiculed, should support the notion that disrespect was not intended nor perceived. Nonetheless, the propensity to combine the profane with the sacred did elicit some moral critique. Otis Green cites the 1567 *Manual de confesores y penitentes* in which Martín de Azpilcueta condemns certain liturgical excesses that were apparently quite wide-spread at the time.

> Here I shall repeat only that Martín de Azpilcueta...states that the admixture of the sacred and profane "is a matter of common practice, that many enjoy it "foolishly thinking that this is permissible, as recreation," and that it is mortal sin only when the song is obscene or those who know better. He adds: "we say the same thing of those who, on Christmas Eve, make obscene replies or call down curses on those who ask their blessing" (Green 1968, 39).

It is upon this turbulent territory that Gil Vicente's *Auto de la sibila Casandra* has acquired its form. As a matter of fact, the very first evidences of Spanish poetry or prose reveal themes in which the secular and sacred battle. *Razón de Amor*, an anonymous poem from the thirteenth-century, contains a debate on the divinity or worldliness--the virtue or vice of Water and Wine.[9] Berceo's *Milagros de nuestra señora*, from the same century, explains through countless examples of miracles, including those granted to an arrogant priest, a pregnant nun, and a devout thief, that all sinners may be saved through simple, yet consistent, intercessory prayer.[10] In this latter work, the Virgin Mary is portrayed as a hearty and formidable opponent of evil who quite literally beats the devil black and blue (Berceo 1968, line 478). Juan Ruiz, an archpriest from the fourteenth-century's *Libro de buen amor*, battles the temptation to pursue worldly love rather than divine.[11] This same work presents the allegorical battle that takes place seasonally between Lady Lent and Don Carnal (Ruiz 1967, 76; 125-127). In due course, similar images and battles appear in the Castilian Theater as well.

The exact genealogy of the Castilian Theater, that is to say, its link to traditions and origins from other countries or regions in Spain, elicits questions. The major obstacle in tracing Castile's theatrical ancestry is the lack of written documentation, for prior to the late fifteenth-century, only one dramatic piece has survived. This is a twelfth-century play called the *Auto de los Reyes Magos*, or *Wise Kings*.[12] For a period of three hundred years, no other theatrical document can be found in peninsular Spain until Gomez Manrique's *Representación del nacimiento de Nuestro Señor* miraculously appears.[13] The latter is a Christmas piece complete with song and interplay between Mary, the female vocalist, and a chorus of nuns.[14] In view of this vast absence of documentation, some critics propose that a systematic and continuous development of the Castilian dramatic tradition cannot be traced without proof or evidence.[15] Humberto López Morales, for example, suggests that it should be sufficient "to analyze just the text itself"...for the text "speaks for itself" (1968, 87).[16] From another perspective, a text may also contain a DNA, a rich heritage that can be traced to an ancestry in other places.[17] From this stance, the monasteries of France, are identified, in part, as propagators, for they brought the liturgical drama, the *Vistatio Sepulchri, Ordo Prophetarum*, and *Officium Pastorum* to the northern region of Spain, Catalonia (Donovan 1958, 6-19; 171).

Manuscripts also identify the liturgical drama in other Spanish regions including Santiago de Compostela, Zaragoza, Granada, and Toledo (Ruiz Ramón 1996, 22-33). During such liturgical dramas, clerics, dressed as shepherds, dance; or sibyls, representing prophets, speak or sing of the birth or death of Christ. Curiously, there is no mention of a site that specifically identifies a liturgical drama in medieval Castile. In due course, however, the Theater appears in *las Castillas* where the terms *representación, auto, égloga, farsa,* or *cuasi comedia* are used interchangeably and refer to a pastoral, religious or allegorical play (López Morales 1968, 220-221).

By the time the Castilian theater officially opens its curtain in history, in 1470, the "deep roots of the medieval and pre-renaissance literary tradition" will have sustained both the blasphemy and piety of the past (Ruiz Ramón 1996, 33). Not surprisingly, shepherd and sibyls, once part of the liturgical Christmas and Eater plays, reappear. The dramatists of this period persist in the parody of the sacred. These dramatist, who were born around 1470, are known as the dramatists of the *Generación de los Reyes Católicos*, referring to the reign of the Catholic King and Queen, Isabella and Ferdinand (ibid., 33). During this period, religious plays are presented in accordance with religious holidays, especially Christmas and Easter. Although these works are not presented concurrently with the liturgy, they are connected intimately to it, and often are presented in holy settings, chapels, or convents.

These dramatists of the early Castilian Theater produce works for the royal court, and their productions are both sacred and secular. For example, Juan del Encina, who is considered the patriarch of the Castilian theater (ibid., 33), creates shepherds who, in one bacchanal *representación*, sing and toast to the pork and bacon and bliss that life brings--so fleetingly--on the eve before Lent.[18] Encina's shepherds are also equally capable of rendering spiritual joy, for they sing and dance before the Christ child on Christmas Eve (Encina 1975, 87-101). And so it continues with the Castilian drama. Religion and the world battle. The sacred and the secular find theatrical space. The pagan and the biblical are juxtaposed. Holiness and virtue are tempered with humor. From Juan del Encina, to Lucas Fernández, Torres Naharro and Gil Vicente, a tradition of scandalous reverence persists.[19]

Very little is known about Gil Vicente, himself.[20] Many of his works unquestionably follow the Castilian tradition and style of Juan del Encina and Lucas Fernández. He was familiar, if perhaps indirectly, with the liturgical tradition of Officium Pastorum and Ordo Prophetarum. Although he was probably born in Portugal and wrote for the Portuguese court under both King Manuel I and his son Juan III, many of his pieces were written in *castellana*. Members of the Portuguese court were bilingual, with the wives of King Manuel, for example, being daughters of Isabella and Ferdinand or the sister of Carlos V of Spain. The language that Vicente used in a play may also have reflected the literary tradition that he followed. Castilian was the most influential language at that time, and the University of Salamanca held a wealth of literary resources. It has been speculated that Gil Vicente studied in Salamanca. Some propose he was theologically trained and knew Latin. What is important, however, is that Gil Vicente, with the *Sibila Casandra*, has produced a fascinating work, an "operetta," complete with dance and song, that presents no disrespect to the church. This *auto*, in fact, is considered to be a type of morality play. Spain, with its rich tradition of a
Theater that questions doctrine or social class, and that can boast of a Lope de Vega, Calderón de la Barca, or Cervantes, can also be proud of Gil Vicente.

And it was with pride in Barcelona, in 1940, that this very play, the *Sibila Casandra*, was revived once again.[21] Vicente's lyrical poems designed for song are supplemented with a musical score written by Maestro Antonio Plenás; and the *auto* is performed on the steps of the royal chapel, the *Capilla Real de Santa Agueda*. The music, photographs, Vicente's text, and the artistic director's preliminary comments to the audience are all recorded in the historical archives of the city (Vicente, 1941). D. Luis Masriera, thus, sets the tone for the play and explains that with Gil Vicente, the "Spanish Theater was born in the lap of our holy mother the Church" (Vicente 1941, 7). He asks that the audience assist in imagining and transporting four centuries past into a perfect illusion. "I see the troupe of strolling players coming," he proclaims. "They are the soul of the festival!" (ibid., 8). He leaves one final warning to those gathered in the patio. "If you want to hear the words of the famous Gil Vicente, be very quiet" (ibid., 8).

The *Sibyl Cassandra* in an Artistic Framework

Gil Vicente's *Auto de la sibila Casandra* is now invoked again--through English to a foreign land, and I offer a similar piece of advice. Be quiet and imagine the presentation of this play. Then transport it, if even just in your mind, to the steps of a chapel, a church, or shrine. To enhance this re-creation, I offer, also, an interpretation of the characters that is based, in part, upon the prototypes that are encountered in the Castilian Theater. Self assured women, for example, appear in Encina's *Egolga VII* and *VIII* where *Pascua* and *Menga* clearly determine their fate (Encina 1975, 180-223). Vicente's *Comedia del viudo* describes the wives of both a widower and his companion as being either strong ideally and morally--capable of managing and correcting members of a household; or strong physically and in opinion and will (Vicente 1968, 128-129; 134-137). Bumbling suitors or shepherds, naive parents, authority honored or challenged, and visits from angels or saints are a mainstay of the Castilian theatrical scene.[22] Thus, it is not difficult to envision the personalities behind Vicente's *Sibyl Cassandra* for they would undoubtedly conform to the comedic, the ethereal or dramatic flair that captured and engaged the court.

The dances, their function, and their steps or style will be more fully explained as well. Apart from this, and the limited stage directions that Gil Vicente himself will offer, the reader and/or the performer or director, as did the Castilian audience, will need to create--or imagine--the rest.[23] The setting evokes a large assembly hall or salon, for as Vicente himself notes, the *auto* was performed in the convent of Xóbregas before Queen Leonor, the third wife of Manuel I and sister of Carlos V of Spain. The costume changes from the courtly to the pastoral are clearly indicated by the dramatist as well and will assist in creating a different scene. The characters' entrances and exits to and from an adjoining salon are most probable. A tableau of the crèche, or Nativity scene, is the only other required element for the setting. As Vicente explains, it is concealed by a curtain which is parted at the climax of the play (Vicente, 1968, 64). Simple paintings or structures to indicate a rustic setting are possible, but not likely. Nor are they necessary. Rustic or palatial environments are defined through the dances that separate scenes, through the costume changes--as mentioned, and are clarified, at times, in the dialogue itself.

Of all of the characters, Cassandra, without question, is the focus of attention. She is not described physically by the dramatist, or in detail through the dialogue; and neither are any of the other characters. She, however, considers herself to be lovely and refined (Vicente 1968, lines 10-12) and, presumably, would possess some of the physical attributes that are, at least, classically ascribed to a desirable young woman.[24] She is, however, also a sibyl, or prophetess. As such, she is associated, in part, with her archetype and the prophecy of the Trojan war.[25] Like her counterpart at Delphi, Cassandra's prophecy--her destiny to be the mother of God---is not taken seriously. As a woman with gifts of foresight, however, she enters, as an intellectual equal, into a theological debate which has been dogmatically set and authoritatively sealed. Ultimately, Cassandra foresees a liberation in which she will not be bound as a servant or bride to either God or man. She will not marry, nor will she become a nun.[26]

Cassandra's suitor, Solomon, is a pseudo-renaissance man, who for most of the play, is portrayed as a fumbling and comedic character. He professes his intelligence, talent, and wealth; yet he is unskilled in matters of debate, dubious with respect to credentials, and unsuccessful with his artistic persuasion. His responses to Cassandra's argument, for example, are not logically based, but instead resort to expressions such as: "I demand that you marry me" (Vicente 1968, line 66), or "I feel that I truly deserve you" (ibid., line 85). His possessions include pine trees, roses, apples, grapes and some thirty-two chickens (ibid., line 262-266). Furthermore, Cassandra is not at all impressed by his skill in the pastoral dance, the latter being a well-known means by which a suitor could influence the course of love (see McGinniss 1997, 17; López Morales 1968, 150). Solomon's lack of tact, confidence, and proverbial wisdom place him at the mercy of Cassandra's relatives, authoritative figures who battle Cassandra on his behalf.

Cassandra's aunts are sibyls as well, and, in addition to their role as an intermediary or matchmaker for Solomon, they function, also, as precursors to Christ's birth and, thus describe and foresee Christ's first and final appearances on earth. Of the three, Erutea is the most accommodating. She is generous with overly positive and sweet advice.

She paints the bright and optimistic side to any dilemma, and reminds Cassandra, for example, that she would not have been born if her mother had not consented to wed. Erutea describes both marriage and Solomon in flowery accolades. Cimeria, on the other hand, is direct and to the point. She offers precise information, does not expect rebuttal, and delivers her opinions in a clear, matter of fact, and unemotional tone. Peresica, by contrast, is a melancholy type, and presents her case with a melodramatic stamp. Her flair for foreshadowing suffering and anguish are reinforced through her facial expressions and her exaggerated gesture.[27]

Cassandra's uncles double as patriarchs of the church. Abraham, who counsels in favor of marriage and family, will sell his point of view through negotiation. He offers bribes, and is willing to present marriage as--well, a bargain. Moses, who has memorized much of Genesis, preaches and corrects Cassandra with somber authority and loyalty to traditional doctrine. Isaiah, a begrudging orator and expert on apocalyptic, relates, with fire and fury, the fate of those, like Cassandra, who presume when they should not.

Angels watch over the Child in the manger and stand guard with humankind on earth. The angels consist of a chorus of four women, presumedly the nuns who form part of the audience, and who, as in Manrique's *Representación del nacimiento de Nuestro Señor*, would intervene in song and interact with the actors.[28] These nuns and, as matter of fact, all of the characters will be graced with skill in both song and dance.

The dances, then, are important features in this *auto*, and should not be viewed as something superfluous. The dances, in fact, are vital indicators of changes of scene or attitude. The *chacota*, for example is danced twice, once by Solomon and the aunts, and later by the characters who approach the crèche. In each instance, the dance itself gives authenticity to the humble and pastoral identity of the characters, and changes a scene from a palatial to a rustic or biblical context. The *chacota* is an unrefined popular dance that is marked by jumps, leaps, stomps, and, in general, by a joyful improvisation.[29]

The *folía* is also a festive dance. The intent of this dance, however, is not just celebratory in nature, for it is traditionally connected with themes of fertility and solicitation. The *folía* is such a wild and fast-moving improvisation that the performers appear enraged or crazy. The *folía*, then, introduces a new scene in which Solomon, accompanied by the uncles, will accuse Cassandra of insanity. As they dance, the men sing , "*Sañosa está la niña,!*" or "The Maiden is completely wild!" (Vicente 1968, line 313-320). Both the lyrics of the song and the style of the dance clearly set both the scene's thematic contradiction and accusatory mood.

A final dance or promenade clarifies the characters' transformation to the palace. As courtesans, they will be educated in the formula of the *danza baja*. This dance accompanies the *villancico*, "*Muy graciosa es la doncella*," and is performed by all of the characters who move with grace and dignity (Vicente 1968, lines 768-78). The courtly dance, especially the promenade, symbolizes joy and service in love. The dance, thus, displays harmony and balance, with both marriage and religious life given equal tribute. That is to say, the tribute to women is particularly evident by the manner in which the dramatist arranges the dancers--in sets of three. A typical dance of that time places the man in the center with two women at his side. The nuns or angels would participate once again, and as the procession unfolds, an angel and a sibyl--women who may serve God in marriage or as nuns, are presented and equally honored and esteemed . Although Cassandra's participation in this dance with Solomon most likely reveals her surrender to marriage; a confirmation of the wedding ceremony, unlike Vicente's *Comedia del viudo* (1968, lines 1038-1055), is not given.[30] This allots the reader or the director some freedom of interpretation, providing that a fundamental function of the *villancico* is not overlooked. "*Muy graciosa es la doncella*," ultimately, is dedicated to Mary who is praised and glorified. Mary is seen as the mirror and model for generations (Vicente 1968, lines 745-746), and is, as Cimeria explains, "God's daughter, mother and wife" (ibid., 747-748). If the worldly is reflective of the divine, this courtly promenade, then, renders a sixteenth-century portrait of the manner in which God may be served on earth.

The *Sibyl Cassandra* with its dance, song, comedic debate, magical metamorphoses, and admixture of psychics and angels, possesses tremendous potential for contemporary appeal. As a result, I have captured the meaning of Vicente's dialogue through an English translation that uses a current conversational style. The translation does not reflect the word order, the ellipses, or the repetitions that are employed by the dramatist to sustain the meter and rhyme of his work. The translation of the songs, however, maintains Vicente's use of *octasílabo*, or eight syllable lines. The rhyme pattern for each verse and chorus is enforced as well. Vicente's use of specific vowels and consonants in a rhyme scheme are observed less frequently, and only when the significance of the text may be preserved.

This translation follows Thomas Hart's edition of Vicente's *Obras Dramáticas Castellanas* (1968). Joan Corominas' *Diccionario crítico etimológico de la lengua castellana* (1954-57) has been used as a basic reference as well. Apart from sources, interpretations, and the technical transpositions, this work attempts to capture the spirit of Vicente's Castilian play in such a way that it may be re-created with the same dramatic flair. This is a task that demands much of the readers or directors for they must envision and juggle the combination of dance, song, poetry, costume, catechesis and comedy that once graced the Castilian stage. Gil Vicente, after all, was skilled in notable ways: as an artist, a dancer, choreographer, dramatist, poet, composer, theologian, historian, and scholar.

With preliminaries and prerequisites for the artistic setting in place, the *Sibyl Cassandra* can be transported, now, into a contemporary mind-set. Thus, a stage that is simple, sparse, yet with room for imagination, may be illuminated. A small rustic structure is situated just to the left of center stage. It incites curiosity, for the entrance to what appears to be a stable is concealed by a curtain that glitters, perhaps, with embossments of heavenly design. From stage right, a shepherdess enters solely and solemnly, and with a sonorous voice, she confesses her grief.

The Play: *The Sibyl Cassandra* by Gil Vicente

The following work was presented before our Lady in the convent of Xóbregas at Christmas Matins. It is about the vanity and presumption of the sibyl Cassandra, for she believes that the prophetic spirit of the Incarnation has overtaken her, and she presumes that she is the virgin from whom the Christ Child will be born. It is for this reason that she refuses to marry. The above mentioned Cassandra enters dressed as a shepherdess saying:

Cassandra

Who is anyone to prevail or insist upon entering into marriage--with me? Well, as God is my witness, I say that I do not want to get married. What shepherd born could be so refined as to truly deserve me? Is there anyone who could possibly compliment me in body, looks, and mind? What woman with acquired polish would gamble with marriage and loose her liberty by allowing herself to be caught, conquered, and always controlled? Who would live exiled in a foreign hand--always in pain, dejected and subjugated? And there are those who actually think that marriage is some great blessing!

Solomon

Cassandra, may God defend you, and I, too, have come in the nick of time for I see that you are distraught. And so our debut, our commencement in love, shall not be detained by me. Well after all, I am here, and it will be well said that I have come because
I am so overcome by you that I believe that our love will come to pass.

Cassandra

I do not understand you.

Solomon

Come now. For you own good, your aunts have been summoned, and soon serenity and joy will be both yours and mine.

Cassandra

What does everyone want from me?

Solomon

That you acknowledge me and take me seriously about this matter of marriage.

Cassandra

For the moment, the only thing that I can believe is that either my aunts or you are delirious.

The Sibyl Cassandra

Solomon

Were we made for one another or not? You can see very well that I am one to be esteemed, and so much so that I swear by my power. If this is not so, then, you owe me not even this piece of straw. I am from a fine lineage with ample provisions. I am valiant, strong, and refined. And although I am presently half run down from having hurried here, still, I beg you...if you would only come to your....

Cassandra

Senses? Without lying in the least, I can truly say that you are out of your mind. And I will not change my mind, even upon the threat of death.

Solomon

Do you not see who I am?

Cassandra

I see you very well.

Solomon

I do not believe you. Can you not love?

Cassandra

I cannot love you!

Solomon

But I am demanding that you marry me!

Cassandra

No, I was first in voicing my demands. I have already said what I desire.

Solomon

What are you saying?

Cassandra
I am saying that you should not talk about marrying me. I do not want to, and I will never consent to marry you--or anyone else.

Solomon
But, do you not want to be with child?

Cassandra
And in that disgrace, do I have to be involved with you? I do not want to be subdued, for I was born to be pure and exempt.

Solomon
But your aunt herself spoke to me and promised a very old-fashioned wedding.

Cassandra
My thoughts are quite different.

Solomon
Well, I still feel that I truly deserve you. It is for that very reason that I came here in the first place.

Cassandra
How nice.

Solomon
Since you do not even care to acknowledge me, it seems to me that you harbor another love somewhere.

Cassandra
I do not want to be engaged or married, nor either a nun or hermit.

Solomon
Tell me what it is that is confusing you? Your anger is wasted on me. Take my advice, or your own when you calm down and really take a look at what you want--logically.

Cassandra
You are wasting time on me. I have already clearly stated my intention.

Solomon
One could easily see into your heart by looking at an enemy.

Cassandra
Do not be so emotional, and do not change the subject. I do not despise you. I was simply born with a destiny that I cannot change.

Solomon
But what would marriage do to you? Leave you in torment, as though you have been robbed of something?

Cassandra
And it is especially for that reason that I reject you and the shortcomings of your sad pleasure. Many marriages are pure purgatory without accommodation or moderation. And if some virtue can be found, marriage still is not a pleasant path. I see all the neighbor women complain about their husbands' peevish qualities. Some men are haughty and boring. Some are cowardly chickens; and others are filled with a thousand jealousies and suspicions--always on guard with sharpened knives. Mistrustful, they are. Jaundiced and cursed by the heavens. Others are like little boys in love, strutting after young chicks with unceasing bribes, insistence and persistence. And the wife! Sighing, and later--at home--complaining and grumbling, and sad because she is trapped. Never would I enjoy my life if I were to consent to such a thing! But of course you are prudent, and you agree with the notion that a woman is weak and like a lamb, skinned, without arms or strength or teeth. And if a husband is lacking in feeling, sense, or virtue? What a waste of girl's youthfulness to be so miserably held bound!

Solomon
I am not like these men, nor will I be. I promise I will place you in a bed of flowers.

Cassandra
And do you think that I can be tricked with little flowers? I do not want to see myself lost, saddened from jealousy or from being spied upon. Scrutinized in public. And this is nothing to be concerned about? Well, best to be not born! And jealousy is the worst because its pain cannot be avoided. Trifles become tempests,

and what is pure becomes tinted another color. Good women are made evil through gossip. Saints become thieves. I do not want to kindle any emotions when I can avoid them altogether.

Solomon

Where there is wisdom and understanding, there is no jealousy, but joy, because wisdom guarantees good fortune.

Cassandra

Wisdom refrains from gambling with luck.

Solomon

Be quiet now, you are suspicious and unenlightened.

Cassandra

Apart from the sweat, labor pains, and crying children, I do not want to see myself in strife simply because you have fallen in love with me.

Solomon

I am going to call Erutea to the village and Peresica and Cimeria and let us see you quarrel obstinately in front of them.

Cassandra

And what can anyone do to me? Who will be the one to marry me at my expense? If I do not want to get married, who is going to force me?

Solomon exits and Cassandra sings.

They say that I must marry, though
I do not want a husband, no.

I would rather live secure
In this *sierra* single and pure
than uncertain about my future
of marrying with a friend or foe.

They say that I must marry, though
I do not want a husband, no.

Mother, I will not agree to marry,
to spend my life fatigued and wary,
or perhaps even waste or bury
any grace God might bestow.

They say that I must marry, though
I do not want a husband, no.

There will not be, nor born is there
anyone for whom I care
for I have become aware
the chosen Rose, am I, I know.

They say that I must marry, though
I do not want a husband, no.

Solomon returns, dressed now as a shepherd. He is accompanied by Erutea, Peresica and Cimeria, and they all enter dancing a *chacota*, and Cimeria says to Cassandra:

Cimeria
What do you think of the lad?

Cassandra
Not good, not bad. I do not want to get married anyway. Who are you to mingle in any plan for marriage? You all know very well that I have something else in mind.

Cimeria
Your mother in her will--now I am not lying to you--arranged for you to get married, because marriage is good.

Cassandra
I have determined my will, and I do not want marriage, nor will I consent to marry.

Solomon
You have received insane council. I feel frightened. How have you become so raving?

Cassandra
In good faith, and from my heart, I swear to you that I do not follow a misguided path. I do not want to give my chastity,
my purity, my innocent freedom, nor my contented spirit
in exchange for a million riches.

Peresica
And if your mother were to have done that!

Cassandra
Go on. What about it?

Peresica
You would have never been born.

Cassandra
I would prefer to select a different and more perfect way of life.

Erutea
Listen, my niece. Right now you have no choice but marriage,
and you ought to take this lad without arguing because he is very good in so many ways.

Cassandra
How is that?

Erutea
He is generous, and virtuous, prudent and well admired. He has land and cattle. He is praised, and he is a fine musician.

Solomon
I have apple orchards, and vineyards, and a thousand pines, and rose bushes just for you to smell. I have villas and other places,
and more than thirty-two chickens.

Erutea
Niece, this lad is genuine. He has been chosen for you.

Cassandra
No, I do not want him, nor did I ask him to be my husband. Protect me Lord from evil!

Cimeria
Do you not see how honorable and reputable he is? How could he be otherwise?

Cassandra
And how would I know if he might change, or what he would do when he finds himself married? Oh, how many single men are there who are pleasant and easy going, then once married, become lions and dragons and veritable devils. If the woman--out of prudence-moves away, they say that she is a lost fool. If she speaks her mind, she is harmed. And this never changes!

Solomon
You are very obstinate. It is probably best that we say nothing more to you until you repent and reject the devil.

Erutea
Solomon, everything could be resolved so quickly, perhaps, if only you would serve her with sweet expressions of love.

Solomon
A maid like her merits favors? Have you not heard her speak?

Peresica
Indeed, Cassandra. Your uncles should come and speak to you. They are learned men.

Cimeria
By God they are. And well-esteemed and sensible.
I know full well that they would end all of this.

Solomon
We shall see what happens, for although she speaks with such malice, she will be fiercely combated.

Solomon exits and returns at once with Isaiah, Moses and Abraham. The four are dancing a *folía* and singing the following song:

The maiden is completely wild
God, who will talk sense into this child?

VOLTA

In the mountain a maid beguiled
will lead her cattle to graze.
Beautiful as the flowers,
like the sea she's wild and crazed.

The maiden is completely wild
God, who will talk sense into this child?

Abraham
I hope that all goes well with you, Cassandra. And as a present, take these two bracelets.

Moses
Let me give you some of my daughters' rings.

Isaiah
I will give you a necklace.

Solomon
And what I would give you, I know very well, but to what avail I do not know.

Erutea
He has many things to give you, dear, as you will see in time.

Cassandra

Am I to be captured by your gifts? You cannot trick me that easily. I have told you already that I have made a promise to myself that I do not have to marry.

Moses

Blasphemy. Marriage is a sacrament. The first one that there was. I, Moses, will tell you about it. I will tell you how it all began. In the beginning God created heaven and earth and everything contained in it. Seas and mountains--out of nothing God made them. The world was a vacuum and empty, and there was nothing for God to love, for the spirit had not created light over the water yet. *Fiat*, and it was done. Perfectly. Sun and moon and stars created clear and beautiful, all of them--according to a just and proper order. Then God gave the sun a partner for a companion. Thus from one light both were embellished with dominance and measure, and each one placed on its own path. Let us make more, said the God the Creator. Let us make a man in our likeness. Angelic in prospect and in strength. And let us create this man from earth. Then God gave him a companion, so that from one grace both were joined. Two in one beloved flesh, as if both were one. And the same one who made them, married them. And thus by his order, God treated marriage as a sacrament that is fixed securely in the world. As a matter of fact, marriage was the first, and it is a determined law. Why are you so obstinate in proclaiming that marriage is enslaving?

Cassandra

What? When man and woman were formed, God spoke of no such thing; no more so than the devil from his altar-piece made and governed each and every day. It was out of pure desire that God united them, and he was not concerned about any other moral standard. And after fate overcame them, all glory died. If I were to marry right here and now, within an hour, I would wish that I had not been born. I have no more than one life, and when it comes to submitting, I say to myself "Cassandra Beware." I do not even dream of a husband, nor do I imagine one. It will not help you to argue because, for me, my marrying is not a matter for discussion.

Abraham
But if you acquire an obliging husband, who never causes suffering?

Cassandra
Never. You are wrong, honorable father, because this would never happen. How can marriage be maintained without suffering and strife? In a minute, contentment can change into contradictory divisiveness. Only God is perfection, and without a doubt, it is true when I say that man is changeable and variable by means of his human condition. And so what I want to say, and what I want to make clear, is that I must remain a virgin because I know without a doubt that God will become incarnate. And a virgin must give birth.

Erutea
I know this very well, and I am certain that the birth must take place in a manger, and the mother remains as virgin as the day she was born. I know that shepherds and villagers will come.
And kings and wise men from the Orient will present themselves to him.

Cimeria
For days I have dreamed and foreseen that I would see a virgin nurse her son who was God made human. And then, later, a vision appeared to me, and I saw her among a thousand young maidens wearing a crown of beautiful stars that glimmered like the sun.
I was left breathless, for never have I seen as glorified and respected of a maiden as this virgin. Nor will her equal ever be created. I perceived her adorned by the sun and armed to fight Lucifer. With her embellished armor, the virgin protected her holy life against evil. She had a cheerful yet militant face. Pleasant, yet radiantly pious. Her modest helmet shone with *Mater Dei* on its crest. And the God child was there, and with a clear full voice, he called to her "Mama" "Mama." And the angels *gratia plena* were truly serene, and each one adored her saying: "flowering rose, illustrious mother from the one who created us, praised be the one who gave us a queen of such holy birth."

Erutea
Peresica, you tell us what you know about this virgin and her birth.

Peresica
Truly, I know about it full well. I am saturated and full of prophecies.
However, they are of pain. In them, the Lord
was being nursed; that is, now and then it appeared
that he did not nurse with pleasure. A cross appeared to him,
and he became frightened, and he cried and sighed. And the mother
comforted him for she did not know about the torments that he saw.
And as he was about to fall asleep, he saw the audacious whips, and
they shook him with fear. And I cannot bear to say anything more
right now.

Cassandra
I presume, and I would swear that from me he is to be born.
There cannot be any one else of my merit, goodness, and noble breed.

Abraham
Again Cassandra rants.

Isaiah
I would say that she is close to being crazy, for sanity is lacking in one
who would profess such a grave discourtesy.

Solomon
The devil must succumb to marriage! By my soul, and by my life,
how could someone so well-informed and well-read become
deceived! Cassandra, your comments lead one to the conclusion that
you are insane, and I Solomon only ask you to agree with me: What
life is there except ours together?

Cassandra
I still perceive that I am she, the chosen one.

Isaiah
Be quiet, you crazy lost soul. Another thing is written about
the chosen mother. As you can very well see, you are the exact
opposite of her because you are haughty, proud, and presumptuous.

And it is in this very matter that you are most dissimilar. The mother of God is without equal, and it is to be noted that she is of humble birth, humble conception, and humble upbringing. The trees and the fields and the forests cry out her beauty—and the snow her brilliance, for she is cleaner and purer than all creatures. Lilies, flowers, and very precious roses attempt to imitate her. Still, there is no star in the sky that can be found more luminous. She was holy before she was born. Preserved. Before she was born, she was chosen eternal queen. Beloved. Kept for the mother of God as a true radiant queen. Generous, with the grace of an empress, but the humility of a noble lady. And even now, there is no one as esteemed.

Isaiah
And her name is Mary, which disproves you from being his mother. And about the son, Emmanuel: butter and honey he will eat, as I predict.

Abraham
I have told you two thousand times that the Messiah will be God alive in person, and I even swear it now by my crown that I am not lying.

Moses
And you also, Solomon, good lad, were given the stories--all prophecies that tell about her and her perfection:

> Beautiful, *mea columba, mea;*
> He who beholds you in sight or vision,
> will leap with joy for having been born,
> and for his strength of youth.

Abraham
If we were to continue to state all that is written about her, it would be an infinite story that the human spirit could not endure. All was prophesied and will be revealed as commanded by the creator of the world. It will be revealed on that profound day. Not tomorrow, but much later.

Isaiah
Africana prophesied about that.

The Sibyl Cassandra

Peresica

And you, brother, spoke about this matter and wrote and documented a sufficient amount for human knowledge. But when the end is going to be, is yet to be known.

Isaiah

The signs I will tell you because I know them. I am certain and well-informed.

Peresica

May God give you a thousand lives! If you tell us, I will reward you.

Isaiah

It will be not far from that moment when God becomes offended, is no longer feared, and is generally forgotten. Then, when loyalty and truth become worthless and despised, the promised forecast will be fulfilled. When the lives of those who follow goodness are demolished; when justice is in malicious hands; when faith is cold--frozen solid--and the holy church is seized by jealous tyranny; when people work to erect too many palaces when the smaller dilapidated ones are left desolate; then, it will not be long. And when people are lost and consumed with shame, and presumption reigns over logic, on that occasion, the world will be lost. And when people falter the most and forget about the end as it may be: At that time a world has been created that must be set on fire!

A curtain opens revealing the nativity scene where four angels are singing:

Ro Ro Ro...
O Child, our God and Savior.
Do not cry, for your behavior,
Pains the Virgin who bore you without labor.

Child, Son of God the Father,
Father of all and everything,
Stop your tears for they will bother
Your mother who should not be crying
For she bore you without pain or woe.
Ro, Ro, Ro...
Do not cause her pain, O no.

So now, Child, Ro, Ro, Ro.
O Child, our God and Savior
Do not cry, for your behavior
Pains the Virgin who bore you without labor.

Moses

In that song I feel certain that our God is born, and he cries because he knows and is quite familiar with the fact that he is flesh like us.

Cimeria

And I too would affirm this and swear that they must be adoring him; and the angels are singing their divine melody.

Isaiah

Well, let us go to adore him and visit the one who is recently born to us. Our two eyes will see the one and only God born to save us.

They exit singing and dancing a *chacota* and arriving at the manger, Peresica says:

Peresica

Erutea, do you see there what I see. The flowering bud has given birth.

Abraham

Oh life of our life. Protected and healed by you, I adore you,
Redeemer. My Lord, God and real man. Holy and divine lamb.
Ultimate great sacrifice.

Moses

O little shepherd born so wise, protect your herd against the hungry
wolves, and have mercy on your feeble flock. O little shepherd,
through the tender human flesh of our sister who sighs with joy, free
us from your anger and heal our souls.

Solomon

What prayer, God, can be made to you? What can be said?
Oh great king, since infancy you are by nature blessed. Infinite
ab eterno capitán. Heir forever of the heavenly empire. As a deity
crowned, let us adore you, human God. And for us, you became a
lamb!

Isaiah

Praises to you, holy Messiah. Now and forever I believe in you. And
with my eyes I see you with such perfection that you fulfill the
prophecies. Child, I firmly adore your sublimity,
and although I deserve no pardon, I state my sin at your feet.
I confess my weakness.

Cassandra

God, I am now lost in this life. I ask you for nothing, because the past
can never be resolved. I never should have been born.
Virgin, mother of God, to you--to you--crown of women
and through your seven joyous mysteries, I ask that you
pray for us.

Cimeria

Mirror of generations and nations. Daughter, mother and wife of
God. Sublime glorious queen. One of a kind. Summit of perfection.
Path through open fields. We run to you sighing, for you will listen
to us. I commend myself into your hands.

Peresica
Oh climax of our world,
Our sole fortune.
Glory of our planet,
Influence in victory,
A reminder,
Our halloed sign.

Isaiah
Ave, stella matutina, beautiful, and dignified. Ave, rose, white flower, you bore the Redeemer, and your radiance, after giving birth, grew even brighter.

After the adoration, they sing the following song that the author wrote and for which he composed the music.

How gracious is the lady,
So beautiful and pretty.

So speak O, you, the mariner
Who lives upon the sea,
Say so if you can see
Boat, sail or star as pretty.

So speak, you, O valiant knight
With arms you dress so gallantly,
Say so if you can see
Horse or weapon as pretty.

So speak, you, O gentle shepherd
Who guards the herd so carefully,
Say so if you can see
A valley or hill as pretty.

It is sung by all the characters, and danced *de terreiro* in groups of three. Afterwards, the following *villancico* is sung:

On to the war,
O valiant knight!
For holy angels fight
To help on earth evermore.
On to the war!

With resplendent sword and arm,
Flying from heaven they descend.
God and country calling them to defend
And keep their people from harm.

On to the war,
O valiant knight!
For holy angels fight
To help on earth some more
On to the war!

Notes

1. This play is contained in *Obras Dramáticas Castellanas*, ed. Thomas Hart (Madrid: Espasa-Calpe, 1968), 43-68. The introduction uses this edition when citing or referring to passages form *La sibila Casandra*.

2. For further information on the *folía*, see Curt Sachs, *World History of the Dance*, trans. Bessie Schönberg (New York, W.W. Norton, 1937), 43.

3. The traditions that underlie the incorporation of sibyls and prophets into Vicente's work are traced by Georgiana Goddard King, *The Play of the Sibyl Cassandra*. Vol. 2 of Bryn Mawr Notes and Monographs. (Pennsylvania: Bryn Mawr College, Lolngmans, Green and Co., 1921). For an extensive survey on origins to this work, see María Rosa Lida de Malkiel, "Para la Génesis del *Auto de la Sibila Casandra*," *Filología*, V, (1959): 47-61.

4. For further information on the *chacota*, see Eugenio Asensio, *Poética y realidad en el cancionero peninsular de la Edad Media* (Madrid: Gredos, 1970), 153 ff.

5. The choreographic design of the dance, sources to the dance, and the parallelistic symmetry of the dance and accompanying *villancico* is analyzed by Cheryl Folkins McGinniss in "The Dance, A Metamorphic Symbol in Gil Vicente's *Auto De La Sibila Casandra*," *Hispanic Review*, 52, (Spring 1984): 166. An example of this type of *danza baja* may be found in Mabel Dolmetsch, *Dances of Spain & Italy 1400-1600* (London: Routledge & Paul, 1949), 25-31.

6. Descriptions of the courtly dance and their symbolic import can be found in Sachs (1937, 277-279).

7. For further information concerning the *auto's* theme of service, surrender, and harmonic balance of the worldly and the divine, see McGinniss (1984, 167-168).

8. Events and influences that shape the spirit of medieval Spain and pre-renaissance Castile are surveyed also in Otis Green, *Spain and the Western Tradition* (Madison: Wisconsin Press, 1968), 3-160; Cheryl Folkins McGinniss, "Perceptions of Transformation and Power: An Inheritance to Encina's Choreographic Plan," *Hispanófila*, 120, (1997): 16-19; Charlotte Stern, *The Medieval Theater in Castile* (New York: Medieval & Renaissance Texts & Studies, 1996), and Stern's article "The Early Spanish Drama: From Medieval Ritual to Renaissance Art," *Renaissance*

Drama, 6, (1973): 177-201. Ovid's *ars amandi*, whether its influence is directly or indirectly transmitted, is also fundamental to early peninsular literary works. This source may be found in *Ovid: The Art of Love, and Other Poems*, ed. T.E. Page, E. Capps, W. H. D. Rouse; trans. J. H. Mozley (New York: G. P. Putnam's Sons, 1929).

9. This poem is a vibrant example of the adversarial contest between virtue or vice (good and evil)—a theme that continues to develop in Spain. The poem is documented by Menéndez Pidal in *Revue Hispanique* (1903): 602-618.

10. For the complete text of "miracles," see, Gonzalo de Berceo, *Milagros de nuestra señora*, ed. A.G. Solalinde, *Clásicos Castellanos*, (Madrid: Espasa-Calpe, 1968).

11. Juan Ruiz's, *Libro de buen amor*, ed. Joan Corominas (Madrid: Editorial Gredos, 1967) is a prime example of the influence of the *ars amandi*. This piece clearly exemplifies the struggle between desire and duty and, in turn, exerts its influence upon subsequent peninsular literary works.

12. The text is reconstructed by Menéndez Pidal in *"El Auto de los Reyes Magos," Revista de Archivos, Bibliotecas y Museos*, IV, (1900): 453-462.

13. The *Cancionero de Gómez Manrique* is preserved in the *Cancionero Castellano del siglo XV*, ed. R. Foulché-Debosc, II, (1915): 1-154.

14. This dramatic interplay is outlined by Harry Seiber in the article, "Dramatic Symmetry in Gómez Manrique," *Hispanic Review*, 23, (1965): 134-35. Seiber suggests that Mary, the female soloist in the *representación*, is joined by a chorus of nuns during the refrain, the *estribillo*, of the song or *villancico*.

15. An ample argument for this position is supplied by Francisco Ruiz Ramón, in *Historia del teatro español (Desde sus orígenes hasta 1900)*, (Salamanca: Ediciones Cátedra, 1996), 21-31.

16. A detailed account of López Morales' corroborative position with Ruiz Ramón may be found in, *Tradición y creación en los orígenes del Teatro Castellano*, (Madrid: Ediciones Alcalá, 1968), 41-87.

17. The development of the liturgical drama and its contribution to the early Theater in Spain is studied and documented by Richard B. Donovan, C.S.B., in *The Liturgical Drama in Medieval Spain*, (Toronto: Pontifical Institute of Mediaeval Studies, 1958).

18. Juan del Encina, *Obras Dramáticas, I (Cancionero de 1496)*, ed. Rosalie Gimeno (Madrid: Ediciones Istmo, 1974), 164-178. For similarities between the Theaters of Encina and Vicente, see McGinniss (1997, 19; 26).

19. See López Morales (1968), and Ruiz Ramón (1996) for more detailed information on various dramatists who contributed to the Castilian Theater.

20. For further information about Gil Vicente, see Ruiz Ramón (1996, 81-83); and Thomas Hart's *Intoducción* in Vicente (1968, x ff.)

21. Gil Vicente's *Auto de la sibila Casandra* in *Representación del Auto De La Sibila Casandra de Gil Vicente* is preserved by the *Ayuntamiento de Barcelona* in the *Museo de Industrias y Artes Populares*, (Barcelona: Archivo Histórico de la Ciudad, 1941). Note, also, that citations of preliminary comments made by the artistic director are my translations.

22. Examples of these prototypes may be found in Encina (1975, 144; 138-145; 166-178; 180-223); and Vicente (1968, 128-129, 134-137; 139). It is common, also, for authoritative systems--church or royalty--to be questioned, as is noted in the example of the bacchanal protest before Lent (Encina 1975, 177); and honored, as is King Juan III in Vicente's *Comedia del viudo* (1968, 155).

23. César Oliva and Francisco Torres Monreal provide an excellent history of the development of stagecraft and scenic art in *Historia básica del arte escénico* (Madrid: Ediciones Cátedra, 1997), 88-180. An additional study of the setting and costuming applicable to Vicente's production can be found in King (1921, 8-19). King suggests that the sibyls wore rich symbolic gowns, often stored by the monasteries specifically for use during Christmas pageants or religious celebrations. Likewise, the shepherds and shepherdesses, dressed in sheepskin, or pastoral attire, or at least carried something such as a hoe or milk pail to designate their identity.

24. A classic example of beauty is described by *Don Amor* in *El libro de buen amor* (1967, 432-445). Attributes include, in part, a small head, blond hair, large clear eyes, small teeth, wide hips, and a long neck. For an additional portrait of beauty, as it would be depicted in Vicente's work, see King (1921, 19).

25. A documentation of sibyls appearing in liturgy or literature is reviewed by King (1967, 42); and Donovan (1958, 165-167).

26. For more information related to marital obligation, see Thomas Hart in, Vicente (1968, xxviii-xxix). See also, Fray Luis de León's *La perfecta casada* in *Obras Completas Castellanas*, ed. Félix García, O.S.A., (Madrid: La Editorial Católica, S.A., 1951), 239-240. Fray Luis' treatise reflects the ideology of the sixteenth century, and it emphasizes marriage as a necessity with virginity and religious service to Christ being a preferred role. His portrait of a "perfect married woman," is that of a women who serves God by caring for her children, governing the household, and obeying her husband. In view of this, Vicente, it seems, is quite bold

in his presentation of the character Cassandra. Her obstinacy provides, at least, a delightful reprieve from the repressive expectations of the day.

27. According to Georgiana Goddard King (1921, 26 ff.), a maximum of twelve different sibyls can be identified in lore and literature. Africana, a sibyl who is briefly mentioned in the *Auto de la sibila casandra* (Vicente 1968, line 606), is loosely associated with the Queen of Sheba, the Shunamite in *Canticles*, and the Lybian sibyl (King, 33-34). Additional information is provided by Carolina Michäelis de Vasconcelos in *Notas Vicentinas, II*, (Lisboa: Ediçäo De Revista 'Ocidente,' 1949), 348-347.

28. See note 14.

29. Sources containing information about all of the dances in this *Auto* (the *chacota*, the *folía*, and the courtly *danza baja)* are identified in notes 2, 4, 5, and 6.

30. The symbolic import of the dance and its visual confirmation of harmony and order is assessed by McGinniss (1984, 167-168).

Works Cited

Asensio, Eugenio. 1970. *Poética y realidad en el cancionero peninsular de la Edad Media*. Madrid: Gredos.
Berceo, Gonzalo de. 1968. *Milagros de nuestra señora*. Edited by A. G. Solalinde in *Clásicos Castellanos*. Madrid: Espasa-Calpe.
Corominas, Joan. 1954-57. *Diccionario crítico etimológico de la lengua castellana*, 4 vols. Madrid: Editorial Gredos.
Dolmetsch, Mabel. *1949. Dances of Spain & Italy 1400-1600*. London: Routledge & Paul.
Donovan, Richard B., C.S.B. 1958. *The Liturgical Drama in Medieval Spain*. Toronto: Pontifical Institute of Mediaeval Studies.
Encina, Juan del. 1974. *Obras Dramáticas I (Cancionero de 1496)*. Edited by Rosalie Gimeno. Madrid: Ediciones Istmo.
Green, Otis. 1968. *Spain and the Western Tradition*. Madison: The University of Wisconsin Press.
King, Georgiana Goddard. 1921. *The Play of the Sibyl Cassandra*. Bryn Mawr Notes and Monographs, II. Pennsylvania: Bryn Mawr College, Lolngmans, Green and Co.
León, Fray Luis de. 1951. *La perfecta casada*. In *Obras Completas Castellanas*. Edited by Félix García, O. S. A. Madrid: La Editorial Católica.
Lida de Malkiel, María Rosa. 1959. "Para la Génesis del *Auto de la Sibila Casandra*." *Filología* V: 47-61.
López Morales, Humberto. 1968. *Tradición y creación en los orígenes del Teatro Castellano*. Madrid: Ediciones Alcalá.
Manrique, Gómez. 1915. *Cancionero Castellano del siglo XV*. Edited by Foulché-Debosc II. Madrid: Nueva biblioteca de autores españoles.
McGinniss, Cheryl. 1997. "Perceptions of Transformation and Power: An Inheritance to Encina's Choreographic Plan." *Hispanófila* 120: 16-19.
_____. 1984. "The Dance, A Metamorphic Symbol in Gil Vicente's *Auto De La Sibila Casandra*. *Hispanic Review* 52 (Spring): 166.
Michäelis de Vasconcelos, Carolina. 1949. *Notas Vicentinas*, II. Lisboa: Edição De Revista 'Ocidente'.
Oliva, César, and Francisco Torres Monreal. 1997. *Historia básica del arte escénico*. Madrid: Ediciones Cátedra.
Ovid. P. 1929. *Ovid: The Art of Love, and Other Poems*. Edited by T. E. Page, E. Capps, & W. H. D. Rouse. Translated by J. H. Mozley. New York: C. P. Putnam's Sons.

Pidal, Menéndez, R. 1903. "Razón de amor con los denuestos del agua y el vino." *Revue Hispanique:* 602-618.
_____. 1900. "*El Auto de los Reyes Magos.*" *Revista de Archivos, Bibliotecas Y Museos* IV: 453-462.
Ruiz, Juan. 1967. *El libro de buen amor.* Edited by Joan Corominas. Madrid: Espasa-Calpe.
Ruiz Ramón, Francisco. 1996. *Historia del teatro español (Desde sus orígenes hasta 1900).* Salamanca: Ediciones Cátedra.
Sachs, Curt. 1937. *World History of the Dance.* Translated by Bessie Schönberg. New York: W.W. Norton.
Seiber, Harry. 1965. "Dramatic Symmetry in Gómez Manrique." *Hispanic Review* 23: 134-35.
Stern, Charlotte. 1996. *The Medieval Theater in Castile.* New York: Medieval & Renaissance Texts & Studies.
_____. 1973. "The Early Spanish Drama: From Medieval Ritual to Renaissance Art." *Renaissance Drama* 6: 177-201.
Vicente, Gil. 1968. *Obras Dramáticas Castellanas..* Edited by Thomas Hart. Madrid: Espasa-Calpe.
_____. 1941. *Representación del Auto De La Sibila Casandra de Gil Vicente.* Barcelona: Archivo Histórico de la Ciudad.
White, James F. 1990. *Introduction to Christian Worship.* Nashville: Abingdon Press.

INDEX

Abraham. *See* patriarchs

Alfonso IX, xi

angels: portrayed as nuns, x, xi, xviii, xix, 21n14

Art of Love (Ars Amandi): display of suitor's talent or wealth, xi, xiii, 8, 10, 20-21n8, 21n11

auto, xiv

Auto de los Reyes Magos, xiii

Azpilcueta, Martin de, xii

battle: as allegory or motif, xiii-xiv; Mary against Satan, xiii, 12; *miles Christi (Soldiers of Christ), 19*

Berceo, Gonzalvo de, xiii, 21n10. *See also* battle

Carlos V (of Spain), xv-xvi

Cassandra: description and destiny as Mother of God, *xvii. See also* sibyls

Castilian Theater, origins to, xiii-xiv, xiv-xv; style, xx

Christ child (crèche), x, xiv, xvi, 1, 12-13; 15-16

Cimeria. *See* sibyls

Comedia del viudo. See Gil Vicente

courtly love, x-xi; expressed in dance, xix, 18

dance, xiv-xv; *chacota*, x, xviii, 7, 16, 20n4; court dance *(de tierra, danza baja)*, x, xix, 18, 20n5-6; in Encina, xiv; folía ix, xviii, xix, 10, 20n2; dance origins, 20n5

Encina, Juan del, xiv-xvi, 20n8, 20n18, 20n22

Erutea. *See* sibyls

Fernández, Lucas, xiv, xv

humor, ix-xii; xiv, xvi

Isaiah. *See* patriarchs

Isabella & Ferdinand, xv; emergence of Castilian Theater, xiv

Juan III. *See* Portuguese court

La sibila Casandra, as *operetta;* performed in Barcelona, xv

León, Fray Luis de. *See* obedience, marriage

Leonor, doña, xvi. *See also* Portuguese court

liberation, viii; liberation theology, vi

Libro de buen amor, xiii. *See also* battle; Ruíz, Juan

liturgy, ix, xiii-xv

Manual de confesores y penitentes: *See* Azpilcueta

Manrique, Gómez, xiii, xviii

Manuel I. *See* Portuguese court

Marriage: as service, xvii, xix; topic of debate, 2-9, 12; as sacrament, 11. *See also* obedience

Mary, ix, x, xiii, 12-14, 16-18. *See also* battle

Masriera, Luis D., xv. *See also La Sibila Casandra*

Moses. *See* patriarchs

Naharro, Torres, xiv

Nuns. *See* angels

obedience, ix, x, xvii, 22n26. *See also* marriage, Cassandra

patriarchs: Cassandra's uncles (Abraham, Moses, Isaiah), ix, xix, xviii; Cassandra's suitor (Solomon), ix, xvii, xviii, 20n3. *See also* dance

Peresica. *See* sibyls

Plenás, Antonio (Maestro), xv. *See also La Sibila Casandra*

Portuguese court (bilingual), xv

Prophets. *See* patriarchs

Razón de amor, xiii

Representación del nacimiento de Nuestro Señor, xiii, xviii. *See also* Manrique, Gómez

Ruiz, Juan. *See Art of Love;* battle; *Libro de buen amor*

sacrament,. *See* marriage

Scripture, ix; as source or paraphrase, (Genesis 1-3), ll; (Song of Songs 2:10," *mea columba mea")*, 14; (Isaiah, cf 1-5; 7:14-15), 14-15; as birth narratives (Luke/Matthew), viii, 12

sibyls, Africana, 14, 23n27; Cimeria, ix, xviii; Erutea, ix, xvii, xviii; Peresica, ix, xviii; counterpart at Delphi, xvii; tradition of, 20n3, 22n23

Sixteenth-century ideology, ix, 20n7. *See also* marriage

University of Salamanca, xi, xv

Vicente, Gil: biographical information on, xv, xvi, 22n20; artistic style of, xix, xx

Villancico, as lyrical song, 18-19

www.ingramcontent.com/pod-product-compliance
Lightning Source LLC
Chambersburg PA
CBHW022016300426
44117CB00005B/226